BR

Bach Cantatas J. A. WESTRUP
Bach Organ Music PETER WILLIAMS
Bartók Chamber Music STEPHEN WALSH
Bartók Orchestral Music JOHN MCCABE
Beethoven Concertos and Overtures ROGER FISKE
Beethoven Piano Sonatas DENIS MATTHEWS
Beethoven String Quartets BASIL LAM
Beethoven Symphonies ROBERT SIMPSON
Berlioz Orchestral Music HUGH MACDONALD
Brahms Chamber Music IVOR KEYS
Brahms Piano Music DENIS MATTHEWS
Brahms Orchestral Music JOHN HORTON
Brahms Songs ERIC SAMS
Bruckner Symphonies PHILIP BARFORD
Couperin DAVID TUNLEY
Debussy Orchestral Music DAVID COX
Debussy Piano Music FRANK DAWES
Dvořák Symphonies and Concertos ROBERT LAYTON
Elgar Orchestral Music MICHAEL KENNEDY
Falla RONALD CRICHTON
Handel Concertos STANLEY SADIE
Haydn String Quartets ROSEMARY HUGHES
Haydn Symphonies H. C. ROBBINS LANDON
Mahler Symphonies and Songs PHILIP BARFORD
Mendelssohn Chamber Music JOHN HORTON
Monteverdi Church Music DENIS ARNOLD
Monteverdi Madrigals DENIS ARNOLD
Mozart Chamber Music A. HYATT KING
Mozart Piano Concertos PHILIP RADCLIFFE
Mozart Serenades, Divertimenti and Dances ERIK SMITH
Mozart Wind and String Concertos A. HYATT KING
Purcell ARTHUR HUTCHINGS
Rachmaninov Orchestral Music PATRICK PIGGOTT
Ravel Orchestral Music LAURENCE DAVIES
Schoenberg Chamber Music ARNOLD WHITTALL
Schubert Chamber Music J. A. WESTRUP
Schubert Piano Sonatas PHILIP RADCLIFFE
Schubert Songs MAURICE J. E. BROWN
Schubert Symphonies MAURICE J. E. BROWN
Schumann Orchestral Music HANS GAL
Schumann Piano Music JOAN CHISSELL
Schumann Songs ASTRA DESMOND
Shostakovich Symphonies HUGH OTTAWAY
Tchaikovsky Ballet Music JOHN WARRACK
Tchaikovsky Symphonies and Concertos JOHN WARRACK
The Trio Sonata CHRISTOPHER HOGWOOD
Vaughan Williams Symphonies HUGH OTTAWAY
Vivaldi MICHAEL TALBOT
Hugo Wolf Songs MOSCO CARNER

BBC MUSIC GUIDES

Brahms Orchestral Music

JOHN HORTON

BRITISH BROADCASTING CORPORATION

Published by the British Broadcasting Corporation
35 Marylebone High Street, London W1M 4AA

ISBN: 0 563 07305 5

First published 1968

Reprinted 1972, 1975, 1978, 1982

Printed in Great Britain by
Spottiswoode Ballantyne Ltd., Colchester and London

Introduction

When Schumann in October 1853, soon after his first meeting with the twenty-year-old Johannes Brahms, wrote a generous article under the title of 'New Paths', excitement at having discovered genius led him to make impulsive statements and to utter bold prophecies. It was unfortunate that he laid upon the shoulders of the young Brahms the responsibility for giving 'the highest expression of the age in ideal terms', a role for which there were already strong claimants, including Liszt and Wagner. Not was he altogether justified in asserting that Brahms was at the age of twenty a complete master of his craft, with no period of gradual development behind or ahead of him. Yet Schumann's often-quoted figure of speech – the image of Minerva springing fully-armed from the head of Zeus – was not entirely inappropriate. In the tremendous piano sonatas, which were among the works Brahms played to the Schumanns on his first visit to their home in Düsseldorf, there was already a driving power and a grasp of large-scale constructive principles that prompted Schumann to call them 'veiled symphonies'; he felt convinced that Brahms would soon find the pianoforte inadequate for his ideas, and expressed the hope that the young composer would 'plunge his magic wand into the forces of chorus and orchestra' and reveal 'even more wonderful glimpses into the secrets of the invisible world'.

By the time of Schumann's death, less than three years later, Brahms had already begun to fulfil these expectations. He soon became an efficient and popular choral conductor, arranged German folk-songs for female and mixed voices, wrote sacred and secular pieces for choirs, and after taking up permanent residence in Vienna in 1863 held for a time the appointment of conductor of the *Singakademie*. It was a choral work with orchestral accompaniment, the *German Requiem*, that set the seal on his reputation as a composer, and other works for chorus and orchestra followed: the cantata *Rinaldo*, the *Alto Rhapsody*, the *Song of Triumph*, and the *Song of Destiny*. The last two were completed in 1871. Up to that date Brahms had attempted very few compositions for orchestra alone; only the two Serenades (Op. 11 and Op. 16), written at Detmold in 1858–9, come within this category, though the D minor Piano Concerto, which went through various stages as a two-piano

5

sonata, a symphony, and finally a work for piano and orchestra, dates from the same period. Altogether, twenty years lay between Schumann's words of encouragement and Brahms's emergence as a successful orchestral composer, an event which can be dated from the performance of the orchestral version of his *Variations on a Theme of Joseph Haydn*[1] in 1873.

Into the next fourteen years, between 1873 and 1887, was packed the creation of all Brahms's orchestral music, both with and without solo instruments, excepting only the two early Serenades and the D minor Piano Concerto. He lived for another ten years after composing the Double Concerto in 1887, but wrote nothing more for orchestra. His comparatively late start in this field was summarized and explained by H. C. Colles: 'He could think orchestrally at the piano, but he could not think apart from the piano. It was to take the next twenty years [after 1853] to make the orchestra his own.' As for Brahms's abandonment of the medium after 1887, this can best be accounted for by the assumption that he felt he had no more to say in it. The Fourth Symphony, his supreme constructive achievement, released him from the discipline to which he had bound himself some thirty years before.

What is so remarkable about Brahms's orchestral music, considered historically, is that almost every note of it (the Serenades being the only exception) has established itself and remained implanted firmly in the concert repertory for almost a century, weathering every school of criticism and every trend of fashion. One obvious reason for its durability is Brahms's well-known ruthlessness towards his own work. From his earliest to his last years he burnt not only drafts and sketches but also whole compositions he thought unripe or unworthy, and he left behind no incomplete works to betray indecision, failure of inspiration, or loss of interest. He was in the habit of submitting each new work to one or more of his friends, not only professional musicians of the standing of Clara Schumann and Josef Joachim, but also accomplished amateurs like the gifted and charming Elisabet von Herzogenberg, at one time his pupil, and the great Viennese surgeon Theodor Billroth. In the end he usually followed the dictates of his own musical instincts, though occasionally he had to be restrained from taking expert

[1] It is convenient to retain Brahms's own designation, although Robbins Landon has cast doubt on Haydn's authorship of the 'partita' in which it occurs.

advice too seriously. Thus when Joachim complained that the broken octaves in the violin parts near the beginning (letter A) of the first movement of the Fourth Symphony were awkward to play, Brahms carefully rewrote the whole passage for nine bars, but Joachim was still not satisfied; it was now, he said, easier for a string player to read the parts at sight, but a great deal of their musical effectiveness had been sacrificed, and he advised Brahms to let it alone after all.

Yet one can all too easily overstress the negative aspect of Brahms's self-criticism. The positive side of it was that in his personality outstanding gifts of lyrical expressiveness, combined with a distinctive rhythmic and harmonic style, were controlled by a highly developed sense of formal proportion, and this is the combination of qualities that has ensured for his work – and more especially for the orchestral part of it – its unique powers of endurance.

Brahms the composer

In an article on Brahms published in 1892, while the composer was still alive, Philipp Spitta wrote: 'The musical politicians of our time call him a reactionary. There could be no stranger accusation . . . Others say that Brahms demonstrates practically that in these [classical] forms something new can "still" be said. Not "still", but *always* this will be the case, as long as our music exists, since these forms are derived from its inmost being and, as far as their main features are concerned, cannot be improved on. Even those who think to have disrupted them and thereby to have performed an act of liberation continue to make use of them, if indeed they are bent on making a satisfactory impression.' The charges refuted by Spitta have often been repeated since his day, and Brahms's devotion to the media of sonata and symphony, classical concerto and chamber ensemble, has been much misrepresented. It is still sometimes regarded as a kind of quixotic determination to 'save' the forms hallowed by Beethoven and his predecessors, or alternatively as a reaction against contemporary trends of which Brahms could not approve, such as rhapsodical construction, the confusion of tonality through excessive chromaticism, and the attempt to produce a synthesis of music with the literary and plastic arts. Supporters of the progressive movements of the romantic period were amazed and exasperated when Brahms seemed unaffected by the influence of a revolution which Beethoven had begun and which was to be carried further by Berlioz, Liszt and Wagner. Hugo Wolf, in one of his articles in the Vienna *Salonblatt*, exclaimed: 'Brahms writes symphonies regardless of what has happened in the meantime.' If Wolf could have foreseen that the next half century was to produce even more radical changes in musical aims, techniques, and fashions, and yet leave the work of Brahms serenely undisturbed in its popularity, his anger would surely have turned to despair.

It is true that Brahms, among all the major composers of his century, had the most scholarly, sensitive, and sympathetic knowledge of the musical heritage of the past. But this was no mere antiquarian interest: the art of Isaak, Palestrina, François Couperin, the Bachs, Handel, was a living part of his experience, and his adoption of an obsolete variation-form in the finale of his last Symphony takes on a new meaning when we recall what he said of the Bach Chaconne for violin alone: 'The Chaconne is in my opinion one of the most wonderful and incomprehensible pieces of music. Using the technique adapted to a small instrument the man writes a whole world of the deepest thoughts and most powerful feelings.'

His bond with the past was even closer, however, because of his innate need for the discipline of form over the expression of feeling and mood, and because of the early training he had received from his composition teacher, Eduard Marxsen. The organic development of themes taken from Mozart and Beethoven had been an important ingredient in that training, and on its basis he imposed his own regular working of contrapuntal exercises, at one time exchanged week by week with Joachim. The art of variation held a particular fascination for Brahms, as it did for Beethoven. The series of large-scale keyboard works in variation form that preceded his orchestral period was to give him great facility in manipulating symphonic material, and the principle of variation informs the whole of his music. No composer is freer from the necessity of making vain and literal repetitions, none is more ingenious in revealing fresh aspects of an idea with which the listener feels himself already familiar. No one of his time, Wagner again excepted, is able to show the same powers of organization in holding a wealth of detail within a clearly-apprehended framework, as Brahms does in the first movements of his Second, Third, and Fourth Symphonies.

Brahms engaged in no verbal exposition, apologetics, or other journalistic exercises in connection with his music; he had no patience with theories about art, and least of all theories about the fusion of the arts. Although he shared to a great extent in the community of interests that embraced musicians and men of letters in the German-speaking countries during the nineteenth century, and was well-read, his attitude towards literary texts was biased in favour of musical considerations. Far from permitting a programme in verse or prose to influence the structure and development of a composition, he treated the poems he set with a high hand, bending them to his requirements in the light of his instinct for musical balance, shape, and climax. At the same time, he learnt from the cadences of verse a flexibility of phrasing that overrode the periodicity of musical time and imparted to his instrumental themes a floating, pulsating character that is all his own. Among the many examples of such melodies that readily occur to mind are the second subject of the Violin Concerto, the second subject of the finale of the Second Symphony, the second (F major) subject of the *Tragic Overture*, the *grazioso* theme of the scherzo of the Fourth Symphony, and the solo cello tune, so rich in rhythmic intricacy within its eight long bars, that opens the slow movement of the B flat Piano Concerto:

EX. I

In his exploration of rhythmic subtleties and complexities, Brahms was even bolder than Schumann, and far more consistently successful. Not all Schumann's experiments in syncopation, mixed metres, and cross-rhythms come off in performance, whereas Brahms never seems to err in making his calculated effect. Displacements of normal accentuation and phrasing across the bar-line produce, as in the examples just mentioned, melodies of moving sensitiveness; while similar devices, when combined with harmonic dissonance, can generate tremendous energy and tension, as in the opening of the First Symphony and in the finale of the Fourth. The *Haydn Variations,* whether in their two-piano or their orchestral guise, owe much of their inexhaustible vitality to the wealth of rhythmic interest they reveal at each rehearing, particularly in the siciliano variation (no. 7), with its mingling of 6/8 and 3/4 and its complex syncopations across the bar-lines, and above all in the great finale where the composer's artistic mastery of procedures such as canon, augmentation, diminution, and inversion, double counterpoint and superimposed metres communicates a marvellous sense of exhilaration. Another outstanding example of Brahms's fluid rhythmic construction occurs at the opening of the Double Concerto, where the combination of duple and triple metres is an important element in the thematic material announced jointly by orchestra and solo cello:

EX. 2

Inseparable from the rhythmic originality that permeates the music of Brahms is his treatment of harmony and tonality. Here there is no question of revolution or even of marked innovation. Indeed, one of the criticisms often made of Brahms's harmony is that, in comparison with the daring explorations made by Liszt and Wagner through chromatic progressions, Brahms is over-cautious in keeping close to a diatonic basis. But he is remarkably skilful in revealing fresh relationships and associations of modes and keys within the ambience of the classical key-system he inherited from Beethoven and Schubert. Although he sometimes appears to be on the verge of a wider, neo-modal range of scale structures, as in the *andante* of the Fourth Symphony, where the modal impression is momentarily intensified by the absence of defining harmonies, he does not in this instance step beyond what can be explained theoretically as a mixture of E major and A minor tonalities. Another passage that temporarily creates an illusion of modal harmony is the solemn four bars for bassoons, horns and trombones near the end of the slow introduction to the finale of the First Symphony. On the other hand, Brahms goes even further than Schubert in bringing about conflicts between major and minor. The opening of the *Tragic Overture* is fraught with dramatic ambiguities, as we shall later observe in more detail, and the beginning of the Third Symphony holds the listener in suspense with its interplay of major and minor thirds and sixths. A more relaxed series of oppositions, which might almost have come from Schubert himself, occurs in the *allegretto grazioso* (third movement) of the Second Symphony:

EX. 3

Brahms's harmonic vocabulary and syntax draw their strength and suppleness from a network of diatonic relationships enriched and adorned with chromatic concords and discords, particularly those derived from flattened degrees of the scale, the whole being embedded in polyphonic textures which intensify accented dissonances and increase momentum. Such passages not infrequently acquire greater tension by being built up over pedal notes, like the drum-beat that throbs through the opening of the First Symphony, or the massively sinking terraces of the opening of the D minor Piano Concerto. Modulations and transitions, some of the finest examples of which occur on the brink of recapitulations in the symphonic movements, are achieved through an elaborate apparatus of pivot notes, enharmonic changes, and the use of varieties of the chord of the augmented sixth. But however bold these may be, there is always clear logic in them, and they keep firmly within the tonal framework of reference; purely impressionistic effects, such as those produced in the writing of Liszt by moving blocks of harmony bodily through degrees of the diatonic or chromatic scale, are quite alien to Brahms. Even the mysterious harmonies in the *andante* of the F major Symphony resolve themselves according to normal late-classical procedures:

EX. 4

Brahms's fondness for key-centres a third apart has often been noticed. It is yet another example of his debt to Beethoven, and governs not only the organization of individual movements but also the planning of large-scale works as a whole. The key-centres of the four movements of the First Symphony rise by a succession of major thirds (C – E – A flat (= G sharp) – C); the two outer movements of the Violin Concerto in D major are separated by an *adagio* whose main key is F; its close relative the Second Symphony is built on a scheme of falling thirds (D – B – G to a return to D in the finale). The scherzo of the B flat Piano Concerto is in D minor. The internal structure of movements in ternary form is apt to be governed by the same principle: the *andante* of the same Concerto has B flat as its main key, but its middle section, in F sharp major, is third-related through its enharmonic G flat. The D major slow movement of the Double Concerto moves to F for its middle section.

A remarkable instance of Brahms's constructive skill is the long delaying action carried out in the exposition of the Double Concerto, from which a quotation has already been given (Ex. 2). Already in the D minor Piano Concerto a sense of ambiguity had been created in the opening bars by sounding the tonic in the bass (D) but straightway turning it into a chord of the sixth, implying submediant harmony. In the Double Concerto the tonic key (A minor) is defined and shown in various relationships, while avoiding any direct statement of the tonic chord in root position until the 57th bar of the movement, when it is heard with the full power of the orchestra. Thereafter it is again avoided for another fifty bars. The whole movement is a wonderful study in key strategy, perfectly matching the intricate problems of form and balance which the composer has set himself in undertaking so unusual a medium.

The tendency to over-emphasize the traditionalist elements in Brahms, and even to deny his originality, persisted almost to the middle of the present century. Thus Peter Latham, in his study of the composer in the *Master Musicians* series, concludes that Schumann was wrong, and that 'Brahms was not to be the prophet of a new age. . . . It was from Liszt and from Wagner that the young men drew their inspiration, the young men who would have the field to themselves in Germany when he was gone – Strauss, Wolf, Mahler and the rest. The still more youthful Schoenberg, who was beginning to compose in the nineties, owes in his early works much to Wagner, something perhaps to Schubert, nothing to Brahms.' While there is an element of truth in such opinions, it is only fair to remember that they have been challenged by no less a personage than Schoenberg himself, in the lecture published under the title of 'Brahms the Progressive' in his *Style and Idea*.

After stressing that the rift opened between Wagner and Brahms by their partisans was historically of transient importance, Schoenberg points out that 'what in 1883 seemed an impassable gulf was in 1897 no longer a problem. The greatest musicians of that time, Mahler, Strauss, Reger, and many others had grown up under the influence of both these masters. They all reflected the spiritual, emotional, stylistic and technical achievements of the preceding period. What then had been an object of dispute had been reduced into the difference between two personalities, between two styles of expression, not contradictory enough to prevent the inclusion of qualities of both in one work.' Schoenberg then refers to the 'Old-Wagnerians' among his contemporaries, 'who considered themselves entitled to look with contempt at Brahms the classicist, the academician'. He claims Mahler and Strauss as the leaders in restoring the balance of justice. Both these men, he says, had been 'educated in the traditional as well as in the progressive, in the Brahmsian as well as in the Wagnerian philosophy of art (*Weltanschauung*). Their example helped us to realize that there was as much organizational order, if not pedantry, in Wagner, as there was daring courage, if not bizarre fantasy, in Brahms.' Schoenberg then goes on to illustrate his thesis 'that Brahms, the classicist, the academician, was a great innovator in the realm of musical language, that in fact he was a great progressive', basing his arguments on detailed analyses of some of Brahms's harmonic procedures and on the prevalence in his works of asymmetrical phrase-lengths. All this may be enlightening to those who find it hard to account for the durability of a body of artistic work which, if its critics were right, must be regarded as belonging entirely to the past and containing no seeds of future growth. The truth is that the instrumental works of Brahms are showing the same kind of agelessness as the keyboard inventions of Bach, the piano concertos of Mozart, and the string quartets of Beethoven.

Brahms and the Orchestra

How did it happen that a composer who, on his own admission, did not think naturally in terms of orchestral colour, who was content, even in his most mature works, with the orchestra as Beethoven and Schubert had left it more than half a century earlier, nevertheless achieved such a degree of mastery over instrumental colour that his popularity in the concert hall and the record shop is not less than that of such brilliant orchestrators as Tchaikovsky, Richard Strauss, Rimsky-Korsakov and Elgar? And by what qualities has Brahms won the devotion of all great conductors since Bülow and of generations of first-class orchestral musicians, despite the technically awkward passages that abound in his scores?

Part of the answer to these questions seems to be that in the long run wholeness of conception, an innate sense of proportion, firmness and clarity of draughtsmanship, and above all an unfailing flow of what must simply be called inspiration, count for more than any instrumental virtuosity. It must be remembered, too, that Brahms made himself a superb master of part-writing, so that his orchestral writing never lacks interest even where its purely sensuous appeal may be limited. This point may conveniently be illustrated from the *Haydn Variations*, a work which, for all its frequent appearances in orchestral programmes, can yield almost as much pleasure when performed in the original two-piano version. Anyone may test this for himself by looking at the piano score of the fourth (B flat minor) variation and attempting to recall the details of its orchestration; only an exceptionally strong memory is likely to bring these readily to mind. Here the composer, being concerned mainly to clarify the two strands of his ingenious and beautiful double counterpoint, provides contrast rather than vividness of colour. It is not unlike organ registration on two manuals, with an independent pedal part represented in the score by double basses. Strings and woodwind, with horns, are interchanged contrapuntally almost regardless of whether the material is equally suited to their capabilities and tonal characteristics, a procedure thoroughly typical of Brahms.

Even what many admirers of Brahms would regard as his supreme moments of orchestral sound often owe less to their actual colouring, appropriate though this may be, than to their architectural positioning, as when the principal theme of the *Tragic Overture* slowly expands in D major minims on horns and trombones at the beginning of the recapitulation, while the violins descend in a chain of suspensions, all above a dominant pedal:

EX. 5

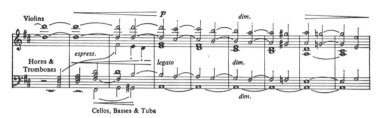

Relationships between texture and colour also must be taken into account. Brahms's lifelong experience in almost every kind of chamber ensemble gave him advantages over all his contemporaries, with the exception of his admirer and protégé, Dvořák. Many passages in Brahms's orchestral writing – in the symphonies, entire movements – have the transparency of chamber textures: an example is the second subject of the first movement of the F major Symphony:

EX. 6

(The melody is then passed on to the oboe, doubled in the octave below by violas, while clarinet and bassoon add a counter-theme, also in octaves; the reiterated E is transferred from flute to first violins, the viola fifths to second violins, and cellos and basses punctuate as before.)

Not only do such passages provide some of the most striking beauties of Brahms's scores, but their occurrence as a relief to denser tracts of instrumentation is one of the most familiar and endearing features of his style, reflecting much that has been handed down about the man's personality, with its contrasts of brusqueness and tenderness, stoical pride and disarming humility.

Too much should not be made of the limited size of Brahms's orchestra. It is true that his contemporary Bruckner, in his later symphonies, demands the triple woodwind, eight horns, and other luxuries of the Wagnerian *Ring,* but Bruckner's is an exceptional case. Tchaikovsky, who orchestrated with greater brilliance on principles quite different from Brahms's, also was content with the standard mid-nineteenth-century symphonic complement of strings, pairs of woodwind (with an extra flute), four horns, two trumpets, three trombones and timpani. Even Wagner in the *Meistersinger* Prelude used the same forces that Brahms calls for in the *Academic Festival Overture,* except that Wagner includes the harp, while Brahms specifies his favourite contrabassoon. The characteristic Brahms sound is due not to the absence of the 'extra' instruments Berlioz and Wagner exploited in their larger scores, but rather to his habitual disposition of the resources he chose to restrict himself to. For example, in his earlier orchestral works at least he is reluctant, as Schumann was, to use the clear primary colours of strings or woodwind alone, and his adherence to the natural horns and trumpets meant that he could seldom let the brass be heard as an independent group. He shows a fondness for doubling string passages with identical notes on woodwind and horns (the sequential crescendo soon after the start of the *Academic Festival Overture* is a fair example), and has frequent recourse to what has been called 'a kind of semi-tutti' produced by strings, woodwind and horns in combination. Another cause of dense texture is his tendency to write in the lower half of the tonal spectrum: he likes solid masses of harmony in the middle and bottom of the orchestra, with alternating notes for violas and cellos (which are constantly divided), backed up by horns and bassoons; and his affection for passages in thirds and sixths, which may be reinforced by woodwind and horns in three octaves, as in the reprise of the first movement of the Second Symphony and the *andante* of the Third, does much to thicken the score.

It should be noted, however, that in Brahms's most mature orchestral works there is much greater interplay of light and shade. It is instructive to compare the finales of the two Piano Concertos. In the earlier D minor Concerto the orchestral part in the rondo is on the whole unidiomatic, and little would be lost if it were played on a second piano, as we know it originally was. In the B flat work, on the other hand, the scoring has a clarity and grace for which the composer has seldom been given full credit. The strings are used alone for long stretches, the woodwind make their distinctive contributions, and in tutti passages the different instrumental families generally keep to their own types of figuration. A similar contrast can be made between the First Symphony, where the woodwind are never allowed to raise their voices independently, and such a movement as the *allegretto grazioso* of the Second, where they engage on equal terms with the strings in animated dialogue. The Third and Fourth Symphonies demonstrate how Brahms had come to realize the marvellous effect of passages for orchestral strings alone. In the Double Concerto, with its problem of balancing solo violin and cello against each other and against the orchestra, the scoring has a translucent quality that differs as much from Brahms's earlier symphonic writing as his keyboard pieces from Op. 76 onwards differ from the three piano sonatas.

The truth is that by the time he came to write the later symphonies (after the First) and the three later concertos, Brahms had a very good idea of the instrumentation that would most suitably clothe his musical thought, and much of his alleged opacity of scoring is far from being the result of ineptitude. The very practices mentioned, like doublings and the weighting of the orchestra in its lower registers, are so closely bound up with the whole character of a work like the D major Symphony that its warm *Gemütlichkeit* would be inconceivable in any other kind of colouring. At the same time, the insight, care, and judgement required in carrying out the composer's intentions are a perpetual challenge to performers and conductors. There is always some new point to be made, some fresh beauty to be revealed by adjustments of balance, dynamics and tempo, and the conductor can always be sure that renewed study and effort will be rewarded by bringing to light some previously unnoticed thematic relationship, touch of colour, or poetry of phrasing. The dynamics of Brahms's scores are a whole field of study in themselves, occupying a place of equal importance with pitch, time-values, and timbre. They may even have thematic functions, as in the example from the Fourth Symphony quoted in Ex. 20. The dynamic markings at the close of a movement are always significant.

In handling the orchestral instruments individually, Brahms draws upon his practical experience of working with them in small ensembles. This is particularly true of the horn, whose possibilities he seems first to have realized through the playing of August Cordes, first horn of the Detmold Court orchestra. The Trio for violin, horn and piano (Op. 40), written for the natural horn, as were all his orchestral parts for the instrument, is but the first of a series of tributes to its magical powers. It is given a prominent place in the first movement of the D minor Piano Concerto, where the rising fourths and fifths of the long second subject, introduced by the solo pianist, seem to cry out for horn tone and are in fact soon entrusted to that instrument in a romantic passage that brings Weber to mind. Other examples are the wonderful horn solo leading to the coda of the first movement of the Second Symphony, and the opening of the B flat Piano Concerto.

The clarinet, which is the only other wind instrument found in the chamber music of Brahms, is equally honoured in the orchestral works. The delightful sound of a pair of clarinets is already realized in the minuets of the D major Serenade, and reappears in the *allegretto grazioso* of the Second Symphony (associated with other woodwind, and again over pizzicato cellos), in the *andante* of the Third, and in the slow movement of the Fourth. Nor can the brief but enchanting dialogue between clarinet and horn near the close of the exposition of the first movement of the C minor Symphony easily be forgotten.

Towards the bassoon Brahms is usually less generous, using it chiefly for complementing woodwind and horns and seldom letting its distinctive voice be heard to full effect; he makes amends, however, in the last of the orchestral works, the Double Concerto, which has some attractive passages for the bassoon, and indeed all the woodwind, in its first and last movements. Some of the oboe's best moments occur in the First Symphony and in the Violin Concerto: it takes the lead in the lengthy opening for wind group in the *adagio* of the latter work. Perhaps the finest passage Brahms ever gave the flute is its poignant solo in the 'sarabande' variation in the finale of the Fourth Symphony. The piccolo has a considerable part, along with a pair of flutes, in the A major Serenade, and in the *Haydn Variations* it not only adds a sharp edge to the contrapuntal lines but also keeps in mind the military associations of the theme.

The trombones, which are absent from the scores of all the concertos, have roles of very great importance in the symphonies. They are used there less often to increase volume than to supply soft full harmony, either on their own or in association with the horns. Their sound is sometimes made to suggest a solemn liturgical function, which is of course part of the historical inheritance of the trombones from the baroque period. In the Fourth Symphony they are held in reserve until they can make their greatest impact, in the grandeur of the passacaglia finale.

Brahms treats the trumpet with little distinction. Only once in the orchestral works, in the *Academic Festival Overture,* does he call for three trumpets, and his refusal to adopt the valve instrument places him under a severe handicap; not only is he deprived of its colour and power in freely-modulating and chromatic passages, but some of his tutti climaxes seem at times to betray inhibitions because of the necessity of keeping the trumpets to their natural notes.

In the Second Symphony and the *Tragic Overture* Brahms employs the tuba to reinforce his orchestral basses when trombones are present, but elsewhere shows a preference for the contrabassoon. Only in the *Academic Festival Overture* are both contrabassoon and tuba included. The contrabassoon is used with particularly telling effect in the *Haydn Variations*, in the first movement of the First Symphony, and in the finale of the Fourth.

The timpani often convey some suggestion of gloom or menace, as in the introduction to the First Symphony, at several points in the D minor Piano Concerto, at the close of the slow movement of the Second Symphony, in the finale of the Fourth, and in the choral works, particularly the *German Requiem* and the *Song of Destiny*. Less formidable, but highly imaginative, are the subdued timpani rolls, followed by soft trombone chords, near the beginning of the Second Symphony, and the triple *ppp* vibration of the B drum over which the clarinets begin to take their farewell of the slow movement of the Fourth – a passage that may have suggested to Elgar the 'departing liner' effect in the *romanza* (Variation XIII) of the *Enigma Variations*. In the scherzo of the Fourth Symphony the F drum has considerable thematic importance during the scherzo. In the same work again, the *ff* reiterations of the E drum in the last two bars of the first movement seem – provided that the conductor does not pause for too long – to be taken up by the initial horn notes of the *andante moderato*. Other percussion is very rare in Brahms: of one exception, the *allegro giocoso* of the Fourth Symphony, he remarked a little shamefacedly that 'three kettledrums, triangle and piccolo will of course make something of a show'. The harp is never used except in the *German Requiem* and a few other choral works, and then only sparingly.

Brahms's long, subtly phrased melodic themes give great satisfaction to string players, even while they execrate the awkward passage-work and accompaniment figures that likewise fall to their lot. Cellists, who seem to have an even stronger love-hatred towards the music of Brahms than have violinists, are called upon for tenor-range melodies and for spreading arpeggios and other forms of accompaniment and filling-in over the rest of the string department. Brahms obviously liked viola tone, and gives his orchestral violas some notable opportunities; their independence is established as early as the coda of the minuet in the D major Serenade, and they oust the violin department altogether in the Second Serenade. Thereafter they are entrusted with such glorious melodies as the second subject of the *Tragic Overture*, on its return in the key of D major, or again at the reprise in the *andante* of the Fourth Symphony, when the violas, divisi, alone are bowed while the rest of the strings shadow them pizzicato – an extraordinary effect which Brahms alone could have contrived.

Both viola and cello sections are often divided in Brahms's scores. Second violins also are occasionally divided, first violins more seldom, and only once – in the First Symphony – is there a solo part for the orchestral leader. The Violin Concerto provides some effective examples of string doubling; there is the breath-taking moment in the reprise of the first movement, when, for a few bars, the soloist duplicates the orchestral violins two octaves higher, and, earlier in this movement, a rapturous 'chamber music' passage with the cellos and first violins two octaves apart:

EX. 7

Incidentally, such passages illustrate Brahms's conservative though always well-judged use of the double bass.

The Orchestral Works

In the notes on individual works that follow, a roughly chronological order will be observed. It must be remembered, however, that a considerable amount of re-shaping affected some of the earlier works, and also that a time-lag of months or even years might occur between the first hint (usually in a letter to a friend) of the beginning of an important new composition and its final completion. The works will therefore be considered in groups according to the stage they belong to in the composer's career, but without regard to strict order of completion or publication.

THE SERENADES, OP. 11 (IN D MAJOR) AND OP. 16 (IN A MAJOR)

Among the independent courts that played so important a part in the development of music in nineteenth-century Germany, that of the Principality of Lippe-Detmold was one of the smallest but also one of the most enterprising. The reigning Prince from about the middle of the century, Leopold III, and various members of his family and household, all had a taste for music which they were able to gratify by employing a permanent orchestra of 45 players, with Kiel, a former pupil of Spohr, as director, and Bargheer, a pupil of both Spohr and Joachim, as leader. Concerts presented by the full orchestra included works by Wagner and Berlioz; a great deal of chamber music was played by the principals, and a choir drawn from the princely household was augmented by selected townsfolk. Clara Schumann was sometimes invited as a guest artist, and gave lessons to one of the Prince's sisters and to the sister of the Court Chamberlain. In 1857, however, Clara removed from Düsseldorf to Berlin, and Brahms, then aged twenty-four, was asked to continue the lessons and to take on other aristocratic pupils, besides conducting the court choral society and contributing as pianist to the concerted chamber music. After a trial visit at Whitsuntide 1857, when Brahms played Schubert's *Trout* Quintet with members of the orchestra, he spent three winters at the court during the years 1857–9, gaining useful experience as a choral conductor and even more valuable opportunities for exploring chamber music. He played through the whole of the classical repertory of trios, quartets and larger ensembles with keyboard, and in a letter to Joachim (17 October 1858) asked for suggestions for 'concertos or septets, nonets etc. with pianoforte. I don't know any beyond the obvious ones. I can make use of wind instruments for all kinds of trios etc.'

To help in meeting this demand, Brahms himself began to write chamber works, and composed his D major Serenade originally as a nonet for flute, two clarinets, horn, bassoon and strings. It might have been better in the long run if it had been allowed to remain in this form. The history of the large chamber ensemble in the nineteenth century has been neglected, but a continuous line can be shown to stretch from the serenades and divertimenti of the Haydn–Mozart period, through the Beethoven Septet and the Schubert Octet, the two Hummel Septets, and Spohr's Octet and

Nonet, to Dvořák's Serenade of 1878, and so on to the twentieth-century chamber orchestra and the virtuoso ensembles with their contemporary repertoire. By turning his Detmold Nonet into a work of symphonic dimensions (the title *Sinfonie-Serenade* is crossed out in the manuscript), though still in the six movements of the original, Brahms made it as he feared into a 'mongrel', too serious in intention to rank as good pastiche but not yet assured and characteristic enough to establish itself finally in the canon of his orchestral music. It seems likely that the pair of minuets (fourth movement) remain in approximately the original scoring, with the two clarinets discoursing in thirds and sixths above bassoon and cello, in company with a flute, a single line violin part, and violas which divide in the coda. For the rest, there are marked differences of style attributable to Brahms's deference to his models in Haydn, Mozart, Beethoven, and Schubert. Nevertheless, personal traits are already apparent. The first movement, perhaps inspired by the finale of Haydn's *London* Symphony (no. 104), leads off with Brahms's favourite solo instruments, the natural horn and the clarinet, and later drops into the combined rhythms he so much affected. The first scherzo grows out of an idea that was later to be developed more fully in the scherzo of the B flat Piano Concerto, while its counterpart in the fifth movement of the Serenade is thoroughly Beethovenish, with reminiscences of the Septet and the scurrying basses of the D major Second Symphony. Between the scherzos comes an eloquent *adagio* where woodwind thirds, and later a beautiful horn call and chains of clarinet sixths, wind their way through a luxuriant growth of string tremolandos and arpeggios. This is followed by the two minuets already mentioned. The high-spirited rondo might well have been inscribed 'Homage to Schumann'.

The D major Serenade, apparently first performed in its original chamber music form under Joachim at Hamburg in March 1859, was given in its revised scoring for full orchestra (with four horns, two trumpets and timpani, but without trombones) a year later, at Hanover, again under Joachim. It did a good deal to advance Brahms's reputation in North Germany, was the first orchestral piece by the composer to appear in the programmes of the Philharmonic Society in London and of the Hallé orchestra in Manchester, and was probably the first of his works to be heard in

Paris, where four of the movements were performed in 1875.

The Second Serenade, in A major, is laid out in an unusual way, for a small orchestra of woodwind, one pair of horns, and strings without violins. The richly sombre colouring that results is reminiscent of Hummel's beautiful Septet for flute, oboe, horn, viola, cello, bass and piano. Brahms was to repeat the experiment of using viola lead in the string section when he came to score the first movement of the *German Requiem*, from which not only violin but also clarinet tone is absent. The new work was sent by instalments to Clara Schumann, who wrote that the opening of the *adagio*, with its majestic ostinato bass, reminded her of Bach: 'the whole movement has an ecclesiastical character – it might almost be an Eleison'. It is curious that the slow movement of the D minor Piano Concerto, written about the same time, should also have been connected in Brahms's circle with a Mass-setting. Brahms derived a great deal of satisfaction from the composition of this Serenade. Indeed, for the first time in his life he felt 'a secret Wagnerian urge' to plunge into journalism and write a detailed note in praise of his 'beautiful opus'. He continued to cherish an affection for it, and as late as 1875 produced a new edition, with changes in phrasing, expression marks, and some of the scoring.

The A major Serenade, even more than its companion, begins to show the breadth of Brahms's imagination. The first of its five movements opens with a Mozartean grace, but cross-rhythms and woodwind thirds and sixths soon reveal the composer's finger-prints. The important second-subject theme with its long sequences of double-dotted crotchets and semiquavers seems related to some of the Hungarian tunes Brahms had running through his head at this period. In fact the whole Serenade is touched with national idioms of various kinds: the scherzo sounds like a Czech *furiant*, and the conventionally-titled *quasi minuetto* must have made the waltz-loving Viennese prick up their ears when they heard the two Serenades, soon after the composer's arrival in Vienna in 1862. The final rondo, one of the most frankly popular tunes Brahms ever turned out, seems to be yet another product of his association with the Hungarian violinist Reményi. We have already noticed the gravely beautiful *adagio non troppo* that forms the middle movement of this varied work, and foreshadows the passacaglia in the Fourth Symphony; the ostinato bass is actually capable of being combined satisfactorily with the theme of Bach's organ passacaglia.

A reason must be found, however, for the comparative neglect of the two Serenades. (The A major one was performed at the Henry Wood Promenade Concerts for the first time in August 1967.) The explanation lies not so much in the unusual forces involved as in the incontrovertible fact that beside the great symphonies, concertos and overtures of the mature Brahms these now appear as little more than apprentice works. Despite many felicities of instrumentation they suffer from monotony of colouring, which is accentuated by the length of most of their individual movements. Brahms had yet to evolve his personal style of orchestration, a process which was to culminate in the orchestral version of the *Haydn Variations*, the work whose linear texture forced him to concentrate on clarity of part-writing in handling a complex score. Structurally also the Serenades seem nowadays too diffuse and long-winded, with frequent recourse to sequential repetition. In this respect, too, Brahms's later craftsmanship in economy of ideas, in their development through organic growth, and in the concealment of the joints in his larger constructions inevitably sets standards which make the Serenades sound at times laboured and contrived. The light and graceful touch which the very serious young composer sought in vain at this period was to come only with middle and later life, above all in the finales of the three last concertos.

CONCERTO IN D MINOR FOR PIANOFORTE AND ORCHESTRA (OP. 15)

To turn from the amiable, period-flavoured Serenades to the tragic D minor Concerto is to leave the shelter of the artificial small court of Lippe-Detmold, in its idyllic country setting, for the harsh realities of Brahms's personal and professional life in his mid-twenties. He had been stricken by the catastrophe of Schumann's breakdown and death, he was baffled and bewildered by his conflicting feelings towards Clara, and he had met with disappointments in his hopes of advancement in his native city of Hamburg.

No other work cost Brahms as much effort as the D minor Concerto, which seems to have taken its origin from the period of the 'veiled symphonies', the titanic piano compositions he played to the Schumanns in 1853. His friends Otto Grimm and Joseph Joachim knew as early as the spring of 1854 that three movements of a two-piano sonata were in existence. Brahms tried it out in this form with Clara Schumann, but told Joachim that the two pianos did not satisfy him and that he would like to put the work aside. Yet in the course of another few months he had scored the first movement for orchestra and sent it to Joachim for criticism, with the diffident note: 'I understand even less about instrumentation than appears from the score: the best parts of it are due to Grimm'. By 1855 Brahms was already describing the work as a symphony, so far in three movements of which the first had been orchestrated; but there must still have been some doubt as to its ultimate form, since in October 1856 Clara referred to it as a concerto. According to tradition the second movement – or from some accounts, the third – was discarded and became the funeral march of the *Requiem*; the present 6/4 *adagio* replaced it, and Brahms wrote above the opening melody in Joachim's copy the enigmatic words: 'Benedictus qui venit in nomine Domini'. This has been taken, rather implausibly, as an indication that the theme was originally part of a Mass. A more probable explanation is that the words were a private tribute to both Joachim and to Schumann himself, whom close friends sometimes addressed as 'Mynheer Domine'. Another theory is that the expression (despite the masculine participle) refers to Clara, and that the whole movement was intended as a portrait of her.

By the end of 1856, Joachim had been sent the rondo to complete the three movements. Already Brahms was feeling at the end of his tether. 'I have neither judgement', he wrote, 'nor any more power over the work. It will never come to anything.' Joachim thought that it might be better to attempt a new finale, rather than to keep working over the old one and losing all sense of spontaneity. He was, however, full of praise for the *adagio*, and with this encouragement Brahms went on revising what had by now firmly settled down to being a three-movement piano concerto. By January 1859 it was ready to be rehearsed with the Hanover court orchestra, Joachim conducting and Brahms playing the solo part, and a few days later came the test of the first public performance in the Leipzig Gewandhaus. It was clear from the first that the members of the Gewandhaus orchestra had formed a poor opinion of the score, and at the performance the audience, containing supporters both of the conservative Mendelssohn tradition and of the progressive New German faction, was openly hostile. Brahms bore his disappointment manfully; he still had faith in the work, was determined to submit it to further revision, and declared that his next piano concerto would be much better.

Some miscalculations remain, despite the combined advice of Joachim, Grimm and Marxsen and Brahms's own efforts; a well-known example occurs in the first few bars, where first violins and cellos are unable to deliver the dramatic initial theme with all the vehemence it seems to demand, though Tovey has argued that the passage represents the composer's intentions quite adequately as it stands. A more serious criticism is the want of relief to the ear that Brahms would have been able to provide if he had been more accustomed to varying the density of his textures, as he did so successfully in his later symphonic works. The *adagio*, lovely though it is, contrasts too little in mood and rhythm with much of what has preceded it, and the finale brings none of the relaxation we welcome in the B flat Piano Concerto. The solo part is written with solidarity and strength rather than with brilliance, very much in the tough, athletic idiom of the early Piano Sonatas in C (Op. 1) and F minor (Op. 5). Even the written-out cadenzas in the second and third movements are terse and restrained; Brahms was to depart from the cadenza tradition altogether in his Second Piano Concerto.

The emotional range of the work extends from classic tragedy to dignified resignation, the latter expressed in such passages as the F major solo (*poco più moderato*) in the first movement, which comes very close to the G flat middle section of the 'funeral march' in the *Requiem*; the two works are, as already noted, historically connected and share a common emotional background. Another point of correspondence can be felt in the poignant sequences of thirds and sixths in the first D minor solo of the Concerto and the setting of the words (in English translation) 'They that sow in tears . . .' in the first chorus of the *Requiem*. Behind both works towers the *St Matthew Passion*, and the spirit of Bach informs the rondo finale, though technically its immediate progenitor is Beethoven's Concerto in C minor. The influence of Beethoven's Ninth Symphony also can be felt in the cosmic immensity of the opening of the first movement. It has often been suggested that this part of the work, if not the whole Concerto, was written under the shadow of Schumann's mental breakdown. Whether this be true or not, one

28

cannot fail to be moved by the involuntary reminiscences of Schumann's music that come through from time to time. The pianist's first long F major solo, for example, to which reference has just been made, almost irresistibly recalls the cadenza of the first movement of Schumann's own Piano Concerto.

Already some characteristic mature structural procedures are fully evident. The principal theme of the finale can hardly be other than a transmutation of the second subject of the first movement, by way of the horn-call and its adoption by the soloist in the octave passage that opens the development:

EX. 8

The work also provides examples of Brahms's masterly key-strategy, as in the diversion created at the moment of return to the main theme of the first movement, where the tonic D minor achieved with almost pedantic orthodoxy by the orchestra is turned into a shattering dissonance by the soloist's conflicting entry a tone higher:

EX. 9

VARIATIONS ON A THEME OF HAYDN (OP. 56A)

For over a decade after the completion of the first Piano Concerto, Brahms wrote no large-scale orchestral work. It was a period of fertility in chamber music, and he was also occupied in choral conducting and composing; his orchestral experience was greatly extended at this time by scoring the accompaniments to the *Requiem* (the performance of which in Bremen Cathedral on 10 April 1868 placed Brahms in the front rank of European composers), the cantata *Rinaldo*, the Alto Rhapsody, the *Song of Destiny*, and the *Song of Triumph* commemorating the German victories of 1870.

On 1 November 1873 the *Variations on a Theme of Joseph Haydn* were performed in Vienna as an orchestral piece. This was Brahms's first purely orchestral composition since the Serenades, and it has remained one of the most popular orchestral works, though some curious mysteries surround it. First, there is the existence of the two alternative versions – two-piano and orchestra – and the fact that each was given half an opus number and evidently regarded as of equal importance, though the piano version is the original. All Brahms's other big sets of variations, including those on a theme of Handel (Op. 24) and the two Paganini sets (Op. 35), had been designed for piano solo, with the single exception of the Schumann variations (Op. 23) which were laid out for piano duet. On the other hand, the D minor Piano Concerto began life as a two-piano sonata, and the F minor Quintet also went through a two-piano phase. Brahms played through the *Haydn Variations* with Clara Schumann in August 1873, and the two-piano version was published almost simultaneously with the first orchestral performance and thus preceded the issue of the engraved orchestral score and parts. Brahms seems to have made it clear that he wanted the keyboard version to exist in its own right and not to be regarded, like the four-hand piano arrangements subsequently made of the symphonies, as convenient reductions of the orchestral score. Brahms himself said that he had a particular fondness for writing for two pianos.

Secondly, there is the theme itself. This is the second movement of the Partita in B flat in a set of six *Feldpartien* long presumed to have been written by Haydn for the Esterházy wind band; its authorship is uncertain. The movement, inscribed *Chorale St Antonii,* is according to Karl Geiringer a traditional Austrian pilgrim song, and some of its companion pieces use similar melodic material in the tradition of the baroque suite. The whole Partita was published by Geiringer in 1932. Brahms based his orchestral version of the theme on the original scoring, which was for two oboes, two horns, three bassoons, and serpent; he uses a pair each of flutes, oboes, clarinets and bassoons, substitutes a contrabassoon for the obsolete serpent, augments the brass to four horns and two trumpets, and reinforces the lowest line with cellos and double basses – another convention of the divertimento or serenade. Violins, violas, and timpani are held in reserve until the first variation, where one of the flutes changes to piccolo. The theme doubtless attracted Brahms through its clear-cut melody and harmony, combined with its unusual rhythmic structure; the first part is made up of two five-bar phrases and is repeated, then follow two phrases each of four bars, then a return to the five-bar motive foreshortened by an overlapping cadence which is extended in all for seven bars, the whole of this second section also being repeated. The reiterations of the final chord are a quaint feature which was carried over into the first variation, where repeated octave B flats provide a rhythmical foundation for the interplay of double counterpoint in duplet and triplet quaver figures.

Brahms must have realized at a glance that the 'Chorale' would make an ideally workable variation theme. Its bass also is admirable, outlining firmly the primary degrees of the scale, but in addition containing a few chromatic notes, including the sharpened fourth which was the accidental Brahms was later to insert in the Bach theme of the passacaglia in the Fourth Symphony. It is possible, indeed, to regard the *Haydn Variations* as in some sense a preliminary study for the last of Brahms's symphonies. There is even a symphonic plan in the grouping of the variations, the first three being energetic, the fourth an *andante* with a change to the minor mode, the fifth to the eighth variations presenting scherzo-like aspects of the theme, and the finale converting it into a ground bass whose cumulative working reaches its climax in a return of the original theme. The variations and finale incorporate almost every conceivable device of contrapuntal ingenuity, together with combinations of rhythms recalling the 'proportions' of the sixteenth-century keyboard composers. Yet no work of its kind has ever sounded less pedantic, and one can only marvel how Brahms emulates and even surpasses Bach, whose *Goldberg Variations* also run the gamut of technical virtuosity while fulfilling their avowed purpose of entertaining the listener.

As a number of points connected with the orchestration of the Variations have already been referred to, it will suffice here to give one more instance of Brahms's increasing sensitivity to instrumental values. The charming *grazioso* variation (VII), in siciliano style, shows considerable originality in the choice of doubling instruments: here it is flute and viola that play the first section of the tune in octaves. Brahms's partiality for the viola again comes out in the finale, when it is heard prominently at the beginning of the canonic entries.

SYMPHONY NO. 1 IN C MINOR (OP. 68)

'After this, in the full sense of the word, incomparable achievement in the field of orchestral composition', wrote Philipp Spitta in a warm letter of congratulation on the success of the *Haydn Variations*, 'your admirers will renew all the more intensely their long-cherished wish for a symphony.' Brahms was now forty – ten years older than Beethoven when he produced his First Symphony, but, as Brahms ruefully observed, the writing of a symphony after Beethoven's Ninth was no longer a joke. Yet he is known to have had three movements of a C minor Symphony in draft for at least a decade before the *Haydn Variations* were completed. There is evidence of this in a letter of 1 July 1862 from Clara Schumann to Joachim, where she quotes the opening four bars of the *allegro* of the first movement – the *sostenuto* introduction was to be added later – with the remark that it sounds 'somewhat harsh, but I have quickly become accustomed to it'. Next, a letter from Brahms to Clara dated 12 September 1868 shows that the finale was already under way. He quotes the horn-theme, adapting to it an extempore greeting introduced by the words: 'Thus blew the shepherd's horn today':

EX. 10

Hoch auf 'm Berg, tief im Tal, grüss ich dich viel tau – send – mal!

Finally, two quiet spells of work in Lichtental and on the island of Rügen in the summer and autumn of 1876 brought the score near to completion. Conductors and publishers – Joachim, Hermann Levi, Albert Dietrich, Max Bruch, Simrock – were all pressing him for a first performance and publication, but Brahms was not to be hurried. On the eve of the first run-through, which took place on 4 November 1876 with the orchestra of the Grand Duke of Baden at Karlsruhe under Dessoff, he was still shortening the middle movements and considering further alterations to the finale. Nor was he alone in his hesitations. Clara Schumann felt disappointed with her first reading of the work, finding it ingenious in construction but deficient in melodic warmth. Other doubts were expressed about the *andante* and *allegretto* which Levi considered, despite their beauty, 'more suitable for a serenade or suite than for a symphony on this scale'. Such friendly criticism, to which Brahms was accustomed and which indeed he invited, troubled him less than the injudicious praise of those who, after the Symphony had begun to make its triumphant way with performances in Mannheim, Munich, and Vienna – all conducted by the composer – styled his First Symphony 'the Tenth' and cast Brahms for the role of the third great B.

Comparisons with Beethoven not only goaded Brahms to anger and derision, but also proved misleading. Any donkey, as Brahms said, could see a likeness between Beethoven's 'Ode to Joy' theme and the C major tune in the finale of his own First Symphony, and in any case it might have been more appropriate to remember that the 'veiled symphony' of his Op. 5 Piano Sonata had opened out into a chorale-like tune in its final movement. Nor is there any close similarity between Beethoven's powerful organic development of terse, seminal motives and Brahms's essentially romantic presentation of his material in complexes of melodic lines and chord progressions, subsequently to be broken down into motives which can be subjected to variation and development.

In some respects this symphony stands apart from Brahms's three later ones. The extraordinarily tense and stressful openings of the first and last movements are the only examples of slow introductions in his orchestral works, and as we know from Clara Schumann's letter, the long *sostenuto* opening was an afterthought, a fact that makes it all the more remarkable that the opening sequence of descending thirds on woodwind, horns and violas functions as a kind of motto theme throughout the symphony; it reappears in second violins and violas near the beginning of the *andante sostenuto* and again on woodwind in the slow introduction to the finale. Other features, unusual with Brahms, can be observed: the high tessitura of the string writing in the slow movement, with its important part for solo violin, an idea that may have been borrowed from the Romanze of Schumann's D minor Symphony; the *pizzicato stringendo* passages in the finale; the almost impressionistic scales that follow; and the string tremolandos accompanying the announcement and continuation of the horn signal. These and other manifestations of the composer's *Sturm und Drang* period, together with an undeniable tendency towards cerebration in the working-out of the finale, associate the C minor Symphony more closely with the D minor Piano Concerto (which, as we know, was earlier conceived as a two-piano sonata and as a symphony) than with the classically-controlled romanticism of the later concertos and symphonies. On the other hand, in the third movement we meet with the first of the distinctive and charming intermezzi with which Brahms had already learnt to relax the severe emotional tension of the symphonic first movement and make it possible to end with a weighty finale. This *allegretto* seems like a pendant to the *Haydn Variations,* not least in its contrapuntal wit: the clarinet, having uttered a five-bar phrase that sounds as artless as a folk-tune (even though it has been suggested that this is but a variant of the oboe melody, answered by clarinet, which has already occurred as second subject in the *andante*), quite unselfconsciously balances it with its own inversion – a pleasantry that is too good to repeat on the return of the tune after the compound-time trio; instead, it is allowed to take another course.

In structural craftsmanship and ingenuity the First Symphony stands up to comparison with any of the later ones, and already we find in plenty those subtle transformations of motives, extending beyond the confines of a single movement, in which Brahms excelled. From the *andante sostenuto,* for example, arise some intriguing questions. Are the chromaticisms of the opening theme derived from those of the first movement? Does the tied quaver-semiquaver figure a little later on find its ultimate destiny in the 'almost impressionistic' passage in the finale? Is the oboe tune a few bars

further on again the origin of the clarinet theme in the next movement? If these are no more than speculations, there can be no doubt
as to contrapuntal felicities like the re-entry of the strings with the
main theme at the climax of the oboe's responsive sentence:

EX. 11

The composer's handling of the orchestra may not show the
confident mastery he was soon to achieve, but this work displays
some effects of colouring found nowhere else. The horn entry in the
finale is a *locus classicus*; no less original, however, is the scoring, a
few bars later, of the same theme for flutes, forte above other woodwind, and brass pianissimo and strings, also *pp*, followed by the
baroque sonority of lower woodwind and trombones. The layout
and dynamics of the whole of this episode, which is too long for
quotation, merit the closest attention. Surpassingly rich, again, is
the scoring of the great C major tune, played on the lowest strings
of massed violins and violas, further enriched by horns and bassoons, over a pizzicato bass. This is neither paper instrumentation
nor keyboard writing transferred to the orchestra, but the imaginative
exploitation of resources whose nature Brahms understood from
practical experience and from working alongside other fine artists.

SYMPHONY NO. 2 IN D MAJOR (OP. 73)

The Second Symphony, though sometimes known as Brahms's
Pastoral, might more appropriately carry the title of 'the Viennese'
since that city took it at once to its heart when Richter gave its
first performance there in February 1877, and indeed preferred it
to the anguished First. The spirit of the *Ländler*, or perhaps of the
Viennese waltz, runs through the opening movement, and especially
the glorious sunny coda. The graciousness and proportion of the
work tend to conceal both its size – it is the longest of the four

symphonies – and also the intricate skill of its workmanship. Once again, the material initially presented is a complex of themes – a chordal melody above a bass motive:

EX. 12

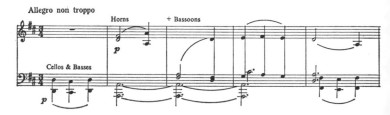

This establishes the home key of D major firmly and immediately, in contrast to the more gradual and elaborate process of key-definition to be observed in the D minor Piano Concerto, the *Tragic Overture,* the Third Symphony, and the Double Concerto. It also soon reveals itself as the propagating cell of the entire Symphony, making its presence known at every turn, often when least expected, as in the slow movement, unmistakably on double basses and tuba just before letter D, and in the repeat of the passage a few bars later.

The D major Symphony belongs to a group of works which includes the Violin Concerto and the G major Violin Sonata, composed during what one imagines to have been one of Brahms's happiest creative periods during holidays at Pörtschach in Carinthia in the summers of 1877–9. The Symphony is not only rich in melodic and harmonic inventiveness, but is also bathed in a mellow glow of instrumental sound of which Brahms alone has the secret. It made an immediate impression of warmth and spontaneity. Billroth expressed this in a letter to the composer (4 December 1877): 'A happy, cheerful mood permeates the whole work. It bears all the marks of perfection, of the effortless flow of limpid thought and warm feeling.' The score seems to be suffused with the stored-up sunshine of those long and richly productive summers by the Wörthersee. Highly characteristic are the passages of thirds and sixths doubled or trebled by the woodwind in octaves; also the piano chords on trombones and tuba (the latter making one of its rare appearances in Brahms's scores); and again, the luscious infilling of the string group with double-stops or divisi passages for violas and cellos. The second subject is given particular warmth through the placing of cellos above violas, accompanied by violin figures which owe their origin to the all-embracing principal theme.

The magical solo for the horn just before the coda of the first movement is something one always looks forward to. Equally memorable is the string passage that follows, with its gentle parody of the Viennese waltz. Another telling feature is the role assigned to the trombones in the first two movements; they are called upon not only for power and energy but also for impressive piano passages, such as the dialogue with the woodwind in the bars preceding (at letter A) the entry of the second D major theme on first violins. It is noteworthy, too, that the heavier brass contribute their quiet sonorities to the slow movement, but thereafter are silent until the later part of the finale. They burst into a veritable blaze of colour in the last five bars, an effect that Dvořák was to borrow at the end of his *Carnival Overture*.

The cellos are again prominent at the outset of the *adagio*, where they are partnered by the bassoons in presenting a dual melody – practically an original with its mirror image, both strands of which undergo variation and development of great luxuriance. The *allegretto grazioso*, already noticed for its serenade-like quality, is a series of free variations, imaginative, most delicately scored, and rhythmically of compelling interest; some of the displaced accents and unexpected groupings of quavers look forward to Bartók's dance-rhythms from eastern Europe.

The finale combines closely knit symphonic organization, based throughout on material which can all be traced back to the initial ideas of Ex. 12, and a relaxed good humour that recalls Beethoven's Pastoral Symphony; indeed, it can hardly be altogether by coincidence that Brahms has given expression to the ripe contentedness of the Carinthian rural scene in much the same tonal language as Beethoven had used in recording his impressions of a convivial peasant gathering. The spirit of Beethoven also seems present in the second subject of this movement, a splendid tune warmed through and through by the lower strings of violins and violas, while the accompanying quaver figure alludes directly to the principal theme and, more subtly, to the germ-cell of the entire Symphony:

EX. 13

The permutation shown in the cello and second violin parts in the bars quoted above is one of the many through which the main subject of the finale can be followed; others involve inversion, metrical transformation (in the triplets of the *tranquillo* section), and the extension of its conjunct elements into passages of scales. There is, in fact, no end to the fascination of detail one can discover throughout this radiant work. Yet the final impression is one of complete spontaneity and total unification.

CONCERTO IN D MAJOR FOR VIOLIN AND ORCHESTRA (OP. 77)

The facile generalization that Brahms tended to produce his works in pairs has caused the first two symphonies to be bracketed together. But, as we have just seen, they belong to different stages of the composer's development; the true companion of the D major Symphony is the Violin Concerto that shares its key and, to quite a considerable extent, its thematic material. Brahms sketched the Concerto by the Wörthersee in the summer of 1878, the year after the Symphony, and at once sent the solo part to Joachim for criticism. Their correspondence shows that the work was at this time being planned in four movements, of which the two middle ones were later to be discarded and replaced by a fresh slow movement. What happened to the scherzo, which Brahms expressly mentions as one of the four movements, is doubtful; Altmann conjectures that it was transferred to the B flat major Piano Concerto, but gives no supporting evidence. The point is not without interest, however, as showing that Brahms more than once planned to include a scherzo in a concerto.

On the whole, Joachim was pleased with the solo part, but confessed that he could not judge the work fairly without a score and without playing it through under concert conditions. Brahms, as usual, urged him not to be too lenient, saying that he would have preferred to go through the work with a less accomplished player to make sure that his demands were reasonable; it was well known that few living violinists could equal Joachim's command of virtuoso double-stops and extensions, and fewer still had his musical insight. Joachim was eager to get his hands on the completed work, but the composer took the rest of the year to finish it. Even after New Year's Day, 1879, when Joachim gave the first public performance at Leipzig, Brahms would not agree to publication. Joachim therefore kept the manuscript score and parts and played the work frequently; he gave it in London at the Crystal Palace in February 1879 and a month later with the Philharmonic Society. He kept on suggesting alterations to the solo part, and even, in the light of experience in concert halls, proposed slight changes in the scoring to make things easier for the soloist: double-bass notes to be omitted, chords to be shortened by rests, and so on. The Joachim–Brahms correspondence at this period is full of discussions about the layout of passages, and the differences between slurs and other markings as pianists and violinists understand them. Joachim's enthusiasm for the work, of which he held almost a monopoly, is shown in a letter he sent to the composer from London in February 1888: 'I have been playing your fiddle concerto and have already given it in Manchester to an audience of 3,000, and next week in Liverpool and Bradford, in each case with Hallé's orchestra.'

This is the last great concerto in musical history to leave the cadenza of the first movement to be extemporized by the soloist. Joachim of course supplied his own, but as other players took up the challenge of the work (a concerto *against* the violin, as Bülow called it) the number of alternative cadenzas rapidly increased. Tovey, in his exhaustive analysis of the Concerto, offers his own solution of the cadenza problem while admitting that Joachim's is 'ideally appropriate'. The problem does not arise with the finale, where Brahms has made the cadenza an integral part of the coda, with an interesting orchestral accompaniment developed out of the semiquaver figures that dominate the movement. It is not only the sheer beauty of the material that captivates the ear in this Concerto, but also its variety. Arpeggio-formed themes, closely akin to those of the Second Symphony, bring out the resonances of the solo instrument and evoke a response from the orchestral horns, while stepwise motives commend themselves alike to the violin and to the woodwind, which are most tellingly used in the openings of the first and second movements. Brahms's mastery of the art of cumulative variation is here applied, especially in the *adagio*, to a solo instrument whose whole nature and tradition have been nourished on variation procedures. The dual character of the violin – its command of expressive monody tending towards timeless reflection, and its physical energy derived from age-long associations with the dance – is fully exploited in the solo part. Lyrical expressiveness is never allowed to impair vitality: the dreamy spell of the cantilena is always broken by the intrusion of some energetic contrast, like the mazurka-like tune that arouses the orchestra to prepare for the soloist's first entry; or (immediately after the mysterious *espressivo* in double-stopping, in the remote key of C minor) the soloist's light but serene dactylic counterpoint to the orchestra, which soon converts the idea into a climax of enormous strength; or the *alla zingarese* of the finale, to whose direction *vivace* Joachim, who understood the gipsy idiom better even than Brahms, added *ma non troppo*.

Not only is the solo part brilliantly written, but its accompaniment throughout shows the composer's judgement and care in details of scoring and balance. As the arpeggios and other display passages assigned to the soloist grow more animated and complex, the orchestral strings are often rested for several bars at a stretch, kept in their lower registers, or used pizzicato, all these being expedients to allow the violin to achieve the pianos and pianissimos at high altitudes which are among the most beautiful and exacting features of the Concerto. The *adagio* exhibits passages of scoring for wind alone, affording relief to the ear and ensuring that solo entries lose none of their effectiveness through competition with the tone of the orchestral strings. A particularly bold experiment is the inclusion of triple-stopping for the solo violin accompanied only by cellos and basses which complete the four-part harmony:

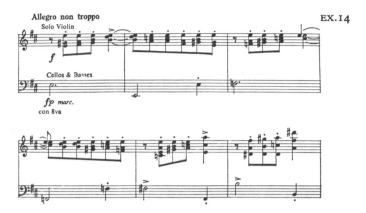

Above all, the Concerto is built round a key-structure whose formal beauty and intricacy can only be fully appreciated from an analysis as detailed as the one Tovey provides. Even without such point-to-point examination, however, one cannot but be thrilled by the adventurous modulations that take place to keys within a radius of a third above or below the tonic; such are the transparently scored F sharp major episode during the development of the first movement and the B flat tutti which balances it on the other side of the tonic, a few moments before the cadenza. The *adagio* also offers a spacious, variegated landscape of key-changes, with excursions to little-explored tracts of enthralling strangeness, making a remarkable contrast to the statuesque tranquillity of the slow movement of the Beethoven Violin Concerto, which remains almost throughout centred in its tonic key. That Brahms should have ventured upon a Violin Concerto in D with the sound of Beethoven's, as interpreted by Joachim, in his ears was in itself an act of faith and courage; that he should have produced one of such originality, sturdily independent of its mighty predecessor yet worthy to stand beside it, is one of the triumphs of Brahms's genius.

ACADEMIC FESTIVAL OVERTURE (OP. 80)
TRAGIC OVERTURE (OP. 81)

Although these two concert overtures were completed at the same time – the summer of 1880, in Brahms's favourite resort of Bad Ischl – and reached the stages of performance and publication together, their provenance is not equally clear. The origin of the lighter work is well enough known; it was an acknowledgement of the award of a doctorate in the University of Breslau in 1879, an honour which had been proposed by Bernhard Scholz, conductor of the Breslau Orchestral Society. The antecedents of the *Tragic Overture* are more obscure.

To deal first with the *Academic Festival Overture*, we should remember that although Brahms, unlike Joachim, never associated himself with a university he was not entirely a stranger to student life. As far back as 1853 he had taken part in junketings at the students' club at Göttingen, where Joachim was attending lectures, and the pair of them had enacted the initiation 'fox-ride' round the common-room table. Brahms had also joined in the singing of student songs at a reception for his friend Billroth at Vienna in 1877.

Brahms described the overture, in a conversation with his biographer Kalbeck, as a *pot-pourri* of student songs in the style of Suppé, who had in fact already composed a set of variations on the 'fox-ride' song. Brahms also made concessions to the popular nature of the occasion by using a larger number of percussion instruments than he ever indulged in at any other time. He even suggested to Simrock that the piece should be made available in a military band arrangement. He could, of course, scarcely avoid making a *Spektakel* with an *ad lib.* chorus for 'Gaudeamus igitur'; had not Weber done the like in his *Jubel* Overture, to say nothing of Wagner in his *Kaisermarsch*? But instinctive artistry, and a genuine sympathy with young people not only for their brashness but also for their vitality, prevailed over any possible desire to undermine the establishment in revenge for its citation of him as 'artis musicæ severioris in Germania nunc princeps'. The result is a most sensitive and disciplined score, with its extraneous material – the initial adaptation of the Rákóczi March (according to Wasielewski, one of Brahms's favourite party-pieces in his younger days), the 'Landesvater' melody, the Thuringian folk-tune to which August von Binzer set his defiant verses on the disbanding of the Jena students' association in 1819 ('Wir hatten gebauet ein stattliches Haus'), the freshmen's initiation song ('Was kommt dort von der

Höh?'), and the inevitable 'Gaudeamus igitur' all fall into place,[1] their banalities redeemed by subtleties of phrase-extension and felicities of orchestration like the 'split-level' violin parts in the 'Landesvater' (firsts remaining poised aloft while seconds continue the tune), viola tone surfacing above the other massed strings, *giocoso* bassoons and oboes in the 'fox-riding' song, and some impressive, restrained use of low-pitched wind – contrabassoon, bass trombone and tuba. Brahms conducted both overtures at Breslau at the beginning of January 1881, the *Academic Festival Overture* being heard on this occasion for the first time.

Writing to Simrock about the overture just completed 'with "Gaudeamus" and all the rest of it', Brahms added that he had not been able to resist satisfying the melancholy side of his nature with a tragedy-overture. He played through this work with Clara Schumann on her birthday a week later, and the first public performance of the *Tragic Overture* took place in Vienna on 26 December, Richter conducting. Kalbeck was responsible for the story that the overture had originated some time before in a commission from the Burgtheater for incidental music to Goethe's *Faust,* and that the two middle movements of the Third Symphony also were originally intended for this purpose. There is also the evidence of Geiringer's discovery, in the library of the Gesellschaft der Musikfreunde, of a sketch-book containing drafts of the *Liebeslieder* Waltzes (Op. 52) and the Alto Rhapsody (Op. 53), among which occurs a sketch of 64 bars of what is now part of the *Tragic Overture.* The passage comes from near the end of the exposition, and is marked in the sketch with a repeat sign – not a normal feature of any concert overture. Part of the sketch is written a fourth higher than the corresponding passage in the *Tragic Overture.* The sketches must date from before 1870, and seem to point to the possibility that the material of the overture was originally planned on different lines and with a different purpose.

Brahms definitely stated that he had never had any particular tragedy in mind. We do know, however, that as a young man he had been intensely interested in classical drama and other literature, spending some of his first earnings as a composer on volumes of

---

[1] In the opening pages occur two fragmentary themes which, though not generally identified as borrowed material, may be recollections of two student drinking songs, 'Vom hoh'n Olymp' and 'Fiducit'.

Shakespeare, Aeschylus, Plutarch (all of course in translation) and Goethe. Plutarch, in particular, gripped his imagination, especially the life of Coriolanus. One of his letters to Clara Schumann dwells on Shakespeare's debt to Plutarch, and how when listening to Beethoven's music 'one imagines that one can see the outline of one of Plutarch's heroes'. We may thus regard the *Tragic Overture* as the outcome of a long-standing admiration for the classical ideal of the heroic, derived both from literary sources and also from Beethoven's *Coriolan* and *Egmont* overtures. Another connection may be felt through the similarities between the style of Brahms's overture and that of his 'Edward' Ballade for piano (Op. 10, no. 1).

The hollow open fifths and quasi-modal harmonies of 'Edward' are present in the dramatic opening of the *Tragic Overture*, but there is something even more powerfully mysterious:

EX. 15

In which direction are those first two shattering chords meant to point? Through a half cadence to D minor or through an inverted plagal cadence towards A minor? And is the pregnant sotto voce theme that follows, like the murmur of a Greek chorus though on wordless unison strings, based on D (modal) minor, or is it A minor after all? There is no certainty until the arrival of the first C sharp, ten bars after the start. Equally disturbing are the frequent rhythmic syncopations, whether of whole sequences of chords or of subdued, restless string accompaniments, or of the touching violin melody of the second subject, with its still more poignant recapitulation by the violas. The warmth of the harmonies at these points contrasts with the starkness of the opening thirdless chords and unisons. We have already admired the classical structure, with the monumental cadence for horns and trombones set at the point of recapitulation like a sculptured pediment (see Ex. 5). The horns, always active and versatile in the scores of Brahms, have important roles to play in this work, notably in the series of octave calls that suggest some rite or ceremony.

CONCERTO IN B FLAT FOR PIANOFORTE AND ORCHESTRA (OP. 83)

As Brahms foretold, his Second Piano Concerto made its way into the world with fewer frustrations and hazards than his First, and it was perhaps a measure of his own satisfaction with its technical assurance that he dedicated it to his strict and revered teacher, Eduard Marxsen. The work had been sketched in 1878, was put aside during the completion of the Violin Concerto, and was finished after Brahms's return from the second of his Italian tours in 1881. At his request, it was first played with the Meiningen Court Orchestra, which had been reorganized during the past year since Bülow's appointment to the conductorship in October 1880, and was rapidly building up a European reputation. Bülow devoted all his talents to making Brahms's music known through scrupulously prepared performances, and there is no doubt that the Meiningen orchestra was one of the decisive factors in establishing Brahms's lasting fame as an orchestral composer. During the winter of 1881–2 Brahms played the solo part in the Concerto in Budapest (the first public concert performance on 9 November 1881), Stuttgart, Zürich, Breslau, Leipzig, Hamburg, Berlin, Kiel, Bremen, Hamburg again with a different orchestra, Münster, Utrecht, and Frankfurt: such was the endurance and mobility of a pianist-composer in the railway age.

It was at this time that Brahms assumed the famous beard, and cultivated many eccentricities. He sent the B flat Concerto to Billroth with a note describing it as 'a few little piano pieces', and told Elizabeth von Herzogenberg that it was 'just a little piano concerto . . . with quite a tender little scherzo'. He also expressed some apprehension about the key he had chosen, lest he should 'milk the B flat cow', which had been so generous to him, once too often: presumably he was thinking of the Sextet Op. 18, the String Quartet Op. 67, the *Handel Variations* Op. 24, and the *Haydn Variations*, all of which share that key. He may also have been mindful that three out of the four movements of the Concerto are in the same key of B flat. To Billroth, who wanted to know why Brahms had included a scherzo, he replied that the first movement was too *simpel* ('plain', or perhaps 'obvious'?) and that 'he needed something strong and passionate before the equally simple *andante*'. In comparison with the turbulent first movement of the D minor Concerto, the first movement of the new work may well have appeared to be sailing too easily towards the *andante* haven. We have seen that the idea of including a scherzo in the Violin Concerto had been considered and rejected. The additional movement makes the B flat Concerto into the largest of all works of its kind in classical form, but it helps to achieve the variety of mood that the D minor Concerto lacks, and the four movements are so well balanced and so full of incident that their length has never been an obstacle to their popularity. The expansiveness of all four of Brahms's Concertos is due to the distinction that he drew between the concerto form and the high tension of his symphonic style. In the concertos, length and leisure are required to give room for the luxuriant variation-technique which Brahms carried over from his solo piano works to his keyboard and string concertos.

Pianistically the B flat Concerto is exacting in the tradition of Beethoven's *Hammerklavier* sonata and Brahms's own early piano works, rather than in the transcendental Lisztian manner, though it makes more concessions, particularly in the finale, to sensuous effectiveness than the composer had allowed himself in the earlier Concerto.

This work alone should be enough to answer the charge that Brahms took over the classical forms and used them conventionally, with little enterprise or adventure in an age that had produced the symphonic poems of Liszt, the programme symphonies of Berlioz, and the music dramas of Wagner. There is little that is orthodox in Brahms's handling of relationships between soloist and orchestra in the first two movements. From the outset, when the orchestra, with the horn as protagonist, begins to set out its thematic propositions, the piano is allowed to assert a right not only to make rhetorical gestures but also to take up ideas as they are thrown out by the orchestra and, even at this early stage of the proceedings, discuss them in its own terms. The assumption of this right is further marked by the absence of solo cadenzas, thus ending the long classical tradition of yielding the floor to the soloist at recognized points in the work. Were it not a contradiction in terms, one might say that the cadenza of the B flat Concerto is to be found at the beginning of the movement instead of in its traditional place near the end. Thereafter, more or less extended passages of unaccompanied piano are interspersed through the Concerto, giving full scope for display, though never being allowed to interrupt the course of organic development.

The orchestra, in the fuller exposition that follows, modulates far more freely than a strict classicist would have thought advisable. Another daring episode occurs after the second subject – one of Brahms's floating, *Lieder*-like melodies – has been quietly dropped into the argument by the orchestra (for the time being in the third-related key of D minor); here it is the turn of the soloist to state the theme in full and build it up into a pianistic episode of such violence as to thrust the orchestra into the background. It is this kind of interchange of traditional roles between orchestra and soloist, combined with the composer's inexhaustible stock of ideas for variation and for bold extensions of the classical key-system, that can be said to revitalize the traditional concerto plan. One more example may be given: the gradual but inevitable approach to the moment when the tonic key returns, with the theme on the horn as before, but this time in a harmonized version, and foreshortened to allow space for a coda which exploits the entire range of the pianoforte in both pitch and dynamics.

Although the germ of the scherzo (*allegro appassionato*) may be found in the D major Serenade written twenty years earlier, this revolutionary addition to the traditional three movements of the concerto is a highly charged amalgamation of sonata and minuet-and-trio forms, showing the composer's fully matured powers of organizing his material. Everything springs from the first half dozen bars containing three motives:

EX. 16

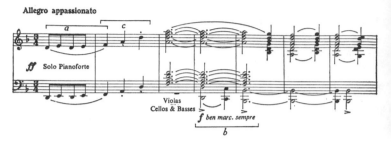

Two of these motives, (a) and (b), form the basis of the second subject whose first presentation with unison strings provides a foil to the pianistic figuration that follows, and from which the solo instrument later derives its pianissimo double-octave passages. Motive (b) has even greater importance. It combines as an inner part with the staccato crotchets of (c) to furnish material for the central section of the movement in D major, where the functions of the classical minuet-trio and of symphonic development are combined. Also, as we have already noticed, it sets up a harmonic tension between the D minor tonality of the scherzo and the fundamental B flat of the entire work – in fact, motive (b) reverses the pitch of the three opening notes of the Concerto. The conflict is only resolved in the first notes of the following *andante*, at the moment when the solo cello sounds its first D above a B flat chord (Ex. 1). More than this, the cello tune at once establishes a direct link with the first movement, since its opening six notes are those of the initial horn-call in a different order. This *andante* is full of enchanting sounds both from the piano, whose figuration explores delicate sonorities a world away from the thunderous trills and broken chords of the first movement, and the orchestra, whose strings are at times divided into no fewer than eight parts.

The rondo is the most carefree of all Brahms's finales, the unflagging humorous invention in the solo part being enhanced by a piquancy and animation of scoring that Brahms never surpassed elsewhere. Had he, one wonders, been looking into the score of *Carmen*, which he had recently acquired and spoke of with much admiration? A sense of lightness is also created by a relaxation of the weight of the B flat tonality that Brahms has hitherto been

48

thrusting forward with so much insistence; this is done by keeping the harmony centred on the subdominant chord of E flat and avoiding a direct statement of the tonic chord until the eighth bar of the principal theme. Rhythmically, this theme is closely related to one already introduced and developed in the first movement, and in its turn gives rise to all the rest of the material of the finale:

EX. 17

The spirit of Hungarian gipsy music which animates the finales of all Brahms's concertos is especially strong in this rondo. It represents an interest that goes back at least as far as the *Variations on a Hungarian Song* (Op. 21, no. 2) for solo piano, dating from about 1853, and continues through the *rondo alla zingarese* of the G minor Piano Quartet (Op. 25) of 1861 and the *Hungarian Dances* for piano duet, which were published in 1869 and from which Brahms orchestrated three numbers for a concert in Leipzig in 1874. His early association with the violinist Reményi probably first turned his attention towards the style. Joachim, who had been a fellow-pupil with Reményi under Joseph Böhm, was himself born on Hungarian soil and may have had Hungarian blood in his veins. It has even been suggested that the rhythmic flexibility of the gipsy fiddlers and orchestras permanently influenced Brahms in his predilection for crossed rhythms and other metrical devices, such as are freely displayed in the finale of the B flat Concerto.

SYMPHONY NO. 3 IN F MAJOR (OP. 90)

The Third Symphony was begun in 1882 and finished at Wiesbaden in the summer of the following year. It was first performed in December 1883 by the Vienna Philharmonic Society under Richter, and met with almost universal approbation. Yet of all the four symphonies it is perhaps the one that least readily yields up its secrets, and from the performers' point of view it sets problems that tax the greatest conductors and orchestras. The music gives the impression of concealing personal meanings. The motto-theme may well be Brahms's emblematic F A F (*frei aber froh*, 'free but joyful'), but the middle term is depressed into A flat, and an ambiguity of mode and a clash of false relations haunt the opening and indeed the whole of the Symphony. Every movement ends piano or pianissimo, the minor third holds the finale in its grip almost throughout, and the close of that movement involves a final disintegration of the main theme of the first movement against sustained major chords, an eerie combination that has already been foreshadowed in the first movement itself. Another disturbing element is the sinister, almost menacing sound of chords foreign to the key and unusual in layout and rhythmic pattern occurring in the midst of innocent-seeming movements like the *andante* and *poco allegretto*. Harmonically this is the most recondite of all Brahms's orchestral works.

From the first, the Symphony aroused speculation. Richter termed it Brahms's *Eroica*, a strange comparison, for two works could hardly be more dissimilar. Joachim confessed that for once he was inclined to stifle his dislike of reading programmes into abstract works, and to imagine in the second (C major) theme of the finale a picture of Leander swimming the Hellespont, his passion urging him on against the raging elements: 'Poor mortal! But how fine and expiatory the apotheosis, the redemption of the destroyed' – a truly remarkable outburst from such a classicist. Clara Schumann was even more romantic in her enthusiasm for a work all of whose movements seemed to her 'to be of one piece, one beat of the heart. From start to finish one is wrapped about with the mysterious charm of woods and forests.' Kalbeck's theory of a connection between the middle movements and Goethe's *Faust* has already been mentioned. Finally, there is the coincidence that the opus number immediately preceding that of the symphony belongs to the setting for chorus and orchestra of 'The Song of the Fates' from Goethe's *Iphigenie auf Tauris* – a sombre cantata, unusual in its vocal and instrumental colouring and full of an agnostic pessimism. It was almost certainly a period of personal crisis for the composer, overshadowed by the deaths of Marxsen and other friends and by an estrangement from Joachim.

This then is a symphony of contradictions – musical ones, like the conflict between the minor third of the motto-theme and the major third of the principal subject that enters above it:

EX. 18

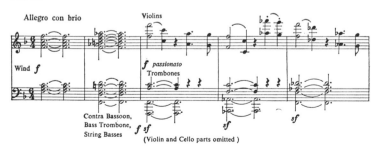

and psychological problems also; and because our age is preoccupied with dissonances, both in art and in personal experience, this may well be the one of Brahms's major works that will continue to exercise the strongest fascination.

The radiantly beautiful second subject is first enshrined in 'chamber music' scoring (see Ex. 6), and indeed the whole work derives much of its sensuous attractiveness from the constantly varying density of the texture. Geiringer shows, from an examination of the manuscript score used by Brahms in the final rehearsals of the Symphony, that he made many minor alterations in the scoring at this stage. 'Such meticulous consideration', observes Geiringer, 'of the slightest subtleties of orchestral colouring belies the thoughtlessly repeated catchword that Brahms was not greatly interested in the problems of instrumentation.'[1] The work in fact glows with rich harmonic colour, some of which has already been illustrated: much of it arises from the exploration of 'flat-side' key-relationships, a remarkable example of which is the transition from the remote tonality of E flat minor to the F major that signals the beginning of the recapitulation; here the conjunction of chords of F, dominant seventh on A flat, and D flat produces a climax of tension:

EX. 19

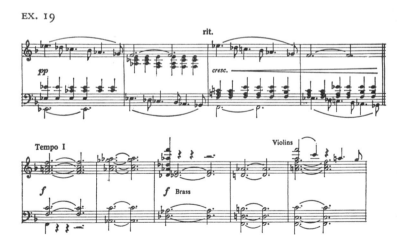

[1] *Brahms, his life and work*, pp. 283–4.

The *andante* starts with deceptive innocence – a diatonic tune like a folk-song, of limited range, the variants and continuations of which (including a casual-seeming transposition of the F A F motto-theme) make up the substance of the movement. The ominous, strangely disposed chords of Ex. 4, however, twice break in, and leave a cloud of apprehension behind them. Once again, it is worth observing the presence of trombones in a movement where neither trumpets nor timpani have a place. The modal ambiguity which characterizes the whole Symphony reappears in the shifting A's and A flats of the final bars of this movement, and produces a cadence of haunting beauty.

A gentle melancholy overshadows the delightfully scored *poco allegretto* which irresistibly brings Schubert to mind, especially in the sequential major-mode continuation of the song-like C minor melody that opens it. The middle section is rich in chromatic harmony to which syncopations add piquancy (the short coda also grows out of this material) and there are some heavenly passages of pure string-writing.

The finale begins under the shadow of the flattened third of the motto-theme, with the key signature of F minor, and unfolds itself as a powerfully built symphonic movement organized round a succession of motives (not melodies, as is more usual with Brahms) until we arrive at Joachim's 'Leander' theme. In the meantime, there has been a striking event in the form of an almost liturgically-sounding chorale, reaching down to the depths of the orchestra with string basses, trombones, and contrabassoon. Tovey mentions that it was Elgar who first drew his attention to the origin of this impressive passage (which gains even greater importance during the development) in a quiet dialogue for woodwind and horns over string chords in the *andante* (letter C). The coda of this movement is full of excitement. First, there is a transformation of the opening theme into a triplet version, in a remote key (B minor) and on muted violas – another example of Brahms's partiality for this instrument. Then, after a transition to F major, the main theme is again transformed, but this time into longer time-values, above which the oboe and horn reintroduce the motto in a slightly extended form (B flat D flat B flat E). Finally, the chorale theme makes its third appearance and is in turn overridden by the motto in its original spelling (F A flat F), while the strings extinguish themselves in the falling arpeggio that complements the motto-theme in the opening movement.

SYMPHONY NO. 4 IN E MINOR (OP. 98)

Except for a narrow escape from the destruction of the manuscript by fire, few hindrances barred the path of the Fourth Symphony to immediate and lasting popularity. It was written in the summers of 1884 and 1885 at Mürzzuschlag in Styria and was tried out on two pianos by the composer and Ignaz Brüll in September. Kalbeck, who was present, was dubious about both scherzo and finale: he could not accept a passacaglia as a fitting conclusion to a symphony. The next day, taking his courage in both hands, he advised Brahms to discard the scherzo, publish the finale as a separate piece, and write two fresh movements to replace them in the Symphony. Brahms, however, stood by his passacaglia finale; if Beethoven had thought variation-form good enough to crown the *Eroica,* it was good enough for him. A private rehearsal, mainly to correct the parts, took place with the Meiningen orchestra under Bülow on 25 October 1885; among those invited to be present were Richard Strauss, then assistant conductor of the orchestra, and Frederic Lamond.

This was Brahms's last work for orchestra with the exception of the Double Concerto written in the following year, although he still had a decade of life before him. The Fourth Symphony is a work of great cumulative power and integrity, a worthy successor to Beethoven's *Eroica* and employing some of its unifying devices. It represents the apotheosis of Brahms's variation technique, and it is fitting that this last great orchestral work should have been foreshadowed by his earliest mature composition for orchestra alone, the *Haydn Variations,* where there is the same progression of interest up to the finale, in which the baroque device of the ground bass sums up all that has gone before. In the E minor Symphony, however, the spirit of the passacaglia makes itself apparent long before it assumes complete control in the finale. The progression of the ostinato theme from Bach's cantata No. 150, *Nach dir, Herr, verlanget mich,* into which Brahms inserted a chromatic A sharp, is already suggested in the harmonic and melodic structure of the very opening bars of the first movement.[1] Even the kind of variation which this initial theme soon undergoes suggests passacaglia treatment in such details as the off-beat bass – recalling the 'divisions' of the seventeenth century – and the fragmented superstructure. It has been shown that the Bach–Brahms ground bass, the main theme of the first movement, and also the principal theme of the *andante moderato*, can all be contrapuntally combined.

Another salient feature of the thematic material of the first movement, which is also apparent throughout the Symphony, is its sequential pattern of falling thirds; almost every bar of the first movement is pervaded by this interval, and as Schoenberg notes in his lecture 'Brahms the Progressive', the reappearance of successions of thirds in the finale 'unveils the relationship of the theme of the passacaglia to the first movement'. This relationship has, however, been exposed from the very outset of the finale, since the passacaglia theme is first of all presented with supporting harmonies on a bass moving downward in thirds. The falling third is equally insistent in the opening unharmonized phrases of the *andante moderato*, and is given even stronger emphasis by the 'Phrygian' tonality of the harmonized continuation. Thirds play a prominent part in the second subject of the same movement, where, Elizabeth von Herzogenberg warned the composer, 'All the cellists will revel[2] in this splendid long-breathed summery song', especially, she might have added, if the conductor insists on slowing down at these points. Nor is the scherzo free from the influence of the same interval; sequences of falling thirds occur, for example, in the string and woodwind passages just before the entry of the second subject (*grazioso*), which is itself partly made up of sequential thirds, and is at one point accompanied by second violin and viola parts that quote almost literally the principal theme of the first movement. Moreover, the entire Symphony is planned on this intervallic relationship, the outer movements being in E minor and the middle ones either firmly in C major, as with the scherzo, or inclining towards that key, as with the *andante*. Finally, there would seem to be a poetical and emotional connection between the E minor Symphony and the third of the *Four Serious Songs* (Op. 121), 'O Tod,

---

[1] The prototype of this theme may perhaps be found in the slow movement of Beethoven's *Hammerklavier* Sonata, bars 80–81.

[2] *Schwelgen.* 'Wallow' might be a more accurate, if less elegant, translation.

O Tod, wie bitter bist du!', which is constructed mainly on successions of thirds distributed over voice part and accompaniment.

Over and above these identities there seem to be still more subtle allusions between one part of the Symphony and another. Thus the figure which appears early in the first movement, accompanied, as we have noticed, with a significant dynamic marking (Ex. 20 *a*), is apt to come into mind when (*b*) is heard in the *andante*. In the scherzo, too, the episode marked *poco meno presto* presents another facet of the same idea (*c*). And a final metamorphosis may be discerned in the *Ländler* (29th) variation in the last movement (*d*):

EX. 20

The *andante moderato* is not only one of the most original and inspired slow movements in all symphonic literature, but also one of the most economically organized. The intricacy of its thematic relationships, both within its own boundaries and extending over the rest of the work, almost defies analysis. Even the first four notes of the horn tune can be shown to have their counterparts in important themes in the other movements, while within the slow movement itself they evolve almost from bar to bar and are implicit in the whole of its material. The process of transformation may be plotted through the following series of outline quotations:

EX. 21

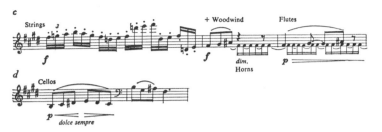

The mighty finale conveys a sense of fulfilment, even conquest. It radiates heroism, the culmination of a spiritual pilgrimage. The words of the chorus on the *ciacona* theme in Bach's cantata are not without relevance: 'Meine Tage in den Leiden/ endet Gott dennoch zu Freuden'.

In this, his farewell to pure orchestral composition, Brahms proclaims himself at one and the same time as (to quote Alfred Einstein) 'the great student of the past, the great initiate into the company of the old masters', reviving a baroque form so strict that the Viennese symphonists had found no use for it; and, as an innovator, grafting it on to the symphonic stock and using the antique form of variations on a ground in a completely original and contemporary manner. Although the ground itself is borrowed from Bach, it is treated in a radically different way from such a work as Bach's C minor organ passacaglia, where from the simplest statement of the ground on the pedals interest is built up gradually. Bach himself, in the cantata *Nach dir, Herr,* uses a freer scheme, the four-bar ostinato being allowed to modulate through a circle of keys, with inversion at one point; some of Bach's violin figuration, incidentally, towards the end of the chorus may have suggested to Brahms details of his own score. In some respects Brahms's concept of the form is related to that of the splendid *rondeau-passacaille* in the eighth *ordre* of François Couperin, whose keyboard works Brahms edited for Chrysander; or perhaps even more to that of the passacaglia, also in rondo form, from Muffat's *Apparatus Musico-Organisticus*, a movement Brahms is known to have admired and studied closely.[1]

[1] Reprinted in Davison and Apel, *Historical Anthology of Music*, ii (London, 1950), no. 240.

Before the Bach theme moves down to the bass, Brahms treats it as a melody in four richly harmonized statements, mainly on wind instruments, above a bass that accidentally or intentionally alludes to earlier movements: its first four notes descend in a pair of thirds, the characteristic interval of the Symphony, and its last three (G F natural E) are the opening notes of the *andante moderato* in reverse:

EX. 22

Similar harmonized statements of the theme occur twice more in the course of the movement, once after the *espressivo* group of variations and later before the coda, thus again recalling the examples by Couperin and Muffat.

Once the ground has reached its normal position in the bass of the orchestra, and the strings have made an effective *arco* entry after their brittle pizzicato introduction, the eight-bar structure of the theme is for some time very little disturbed; but presently, as in the *Haydn Variations*, a scheme of groupings begins to be revealed. The first indication of such a plan occurs after a pointed hesitation in the bass, followed by a doubling of the time (3/4 becomes 3/2) and the start of a sarabande-like interlude comprising four variations. The first of these arrests attention by the eloquent, improvisatory character of the solo for flute, the last two by the solemn chords allotted to woodwind and brass (Ex. 23 *a*). At this point the listener (rather than the score-follower) may experience a *frisson* of half-recognition, which on further investigation can be traced to a similarity of harmonic outline between the wind chords and a passage in the preceding scherzo (Ex. 23 *b*):

EX. 23

a   Trombones, Bassoons and Horns: String figures omitted

b Trumpets, Horns, Basses, etc. String figures omitted.

But as we shall see presently, the connection between these two movements is about to be established even more dramatically.

The beginning of a third stage of the movement is marked by a near-repetition of the harmonized theme as heard at the outset, but with a wry twist at the end that momentarily jerks it out of its key. This is the starting-point for a series of tutti variations, relieved by some scherzo-like treatment with sequences of falling thirds and animated triplet rhythms, and again by smooth horn and woodwind sequences. A climax is indicated by a slowing down of both tempo and harmonic progression, and then follows (in quicker tempo) a coda filled with fresh surprises. First, the A sharp Brahms added to Bach's theme is re-spelt B flat, which at once gives rise to some thrilling harmonic possibilities. Their full realization involves a canon between top and bottom of the orchestra, with the bass always following at two bars' distance and a semitone higher, the result being a series of enharmonic progressions stretching the tonal system to its extreme limits. The emotional impact of this event, wrenching the hearer violently away from the E minor–major centre to which he has been securely anchored, can only be compared with the almost terrifying effect of the chromatic fugal stretto that takes place in the finale of Mozart's *Jupiter* Symphony.

But Brahms has yet another powerful stroke in reserve, and one that seems generally to have escaped comment. This takes the form of a musical counterpart to the dramatic irony of the tragic stage, and occurs when the trombones, elbowing their way up with a diminished version of the ground, become involved along with the timpani in a violent collision with the rest of the orchestra which is plunging downwards on to a chord of F – a chord almost identical in position and instrumentation with the one previously used to comic effect in the scherzo, but here taken in grim earnest. The reappearance of a vivid chord of the augmented sixth in the same context, including a resolution on to C major, leaves the allusion in no doubt:

EX. 24

This powerful diversion brings about a final modulation back to the tonic key and an exultant ending to what must be accounted the greatest symphonic work since Schubert's great C major, perhaps since Beethoven's Ninth.

CONCERTO IN A MINOR FOR VIOLIN, VIOLONCELLO AND ORCHESTRA (OP. 102)

After completing the Fourth Symphony, Brahms concentrated mainly on chamber music, and during a long summer spent at Thun, in Switzerland, near the home of his friend the poet Widmann, he produced the F major Cello Sonata (Op. 99), the A major Violin Sonata (Op. 100), and the C minor Trio for violin, cello and piano (Op. 101). It is possible that this series of works, and especially the Trio, gave Brahms the idea of combining violin and violoncello in a concerto. As usual, he first tested the reactions of his friends. To Clara Schumann he wrote: 'I ought to have passed on the idea to someone who knows the fiddle better than I do (Joachim, unfortunately, has given up composing). It is quite a different matter to write for instruments whose nature and sound one has only approximately in one's head, and hears only in imagination, rather than to write for an instrument one knows thoroughly, as I do the piano.' Clara reassured him at once by saying that his symphonies and string sonatas must have given him ample confidence in his ability to entice unimagined beauties from them. Brahms's motives for telling Joachim about the proposed new concerto were more complex. From the first he had intended the solo parts for him and for Robert Hausmann, the cellist of the Joachim Quartet, and he inevitably looked to both of them for technical advice. But he was also trying to repair the personal friendship that had been shattered by Brahms's clumsy though well-meant intervention in Joachim's domestic affairs, and he must have hoped that a series of professional meetings to work on the new concerto might lead to a patching up of the quarrel. Joachim had never wavered in his admiration for Brahms's music, however much he had been provoked by his manners, and both Joachim and Hausmann seized enthusiastically upon the solo parts Brahms sent to them from Switzerland. At length they all came together. Rehearsals with piano took place on 21 and 22 September at Clara Schumann's house in Baden-Baden, and on the 23rd the Concerto was played through with the orchestra of the Kursaal. 'This concerto', Clara wrote in her diary, 'is in some degree a work of reconciliation – Joachim and Brahms have spoken to each other for the first time for years.' On the professional side, the two string experts offered various suggestions for improving the solo parts, some of which remain pencilled in Joachim's handwriting in the manuscript score (reproduced in Geiringer's book on the composer). True to his independent principles, however, Brahms declined to incorporate all these alterations in the final published version. The first public performance of the Concerto took place at Cologne on 18 October 1887 with the composer conducting.

Two solo instruments covering as wide a range of pitch and expression as the violin and violoncello are capable of creating full and satisfying harmony between them for long passages, as Brahms had recently demonstrated in the *andante grazioso* of the C minor Trio, and demand much scope and independence in a work of concerto type. This is made clear in the first half dozen bars of the Double Concerto (see Ex. 2). What seems like the beginning of a normal orchestral exposition (though initially outside the tonic key) on the part of the orchestra is imperiously broken off by the unaccompanied solo cello (which, it is worth noting, tends to take the lead throughout the Concerto) with a free commentary on the theme the orchestra has begun to enunciate. An attempt on the part of the woodwind to introduce a second theme (in A major, over a dominant pedal) is similarly interrupted by the solo violin, and both soloists then ruminate on some of the ideas so far thrown out, until they combine in a cadenza-like rush of arpeggios and scales. Other aspects of this remarkable exordium have already been discussed on p. 13. The orchestra is now permitted to start its exposition in earnest, and leads by way of an important syncopated, dissonant passage to the second subject. Rhythmically this is almost identical with the opening tutti of J. B. Viotti's Violin Concerto No. 22 in A minor, a favourite work of both Joachim and Brahms and alluded to here, one imagines, as part of the process of reconciliation:

EX. 25

a VIOTTI, Violin Concerto No. 22

b BRAHMS, Op. 102

f *ben marc.*

This orchestral tutti again is clearly punctuated, and is followed by the soloists, with the cello again in the lead, discussing both first and second subjects, linked with an idea of their own in triplet quavers, derived without doubt for the triplet-crotchet figures in the introductory bars of the movement (see Ex. 2). In the course of the development the virtuoso possibilities of the solo instruments – multiple stopping, rapid simultaneous triplets and scale passages in octaves, chains of trills, and arpeggios across the strings – are thrown into prominence by a reticent use of the orchestra. Much of the arpeggio figuration in this movement, and still more in the finale, is really pianistic in idiom and belongs to the delicate, almost impressionistic style of Brahms's last-period piano pieces; it is, however, adapted in such a way that it takes on the character of virtuoso string writing. The importance of the syncopated, dissonant theme already referred to becomes more clearly apparent at this stage, though all its implications are not to be realized until the last movement.

There is never anything perfunctory about Brahms's first-movement recapitulations, and in this instance his ingenuity is fully exercised to allow the soloists fresh opportunities both technical and expressive, as in their surpassingly beautiful treatment of the lyrical second subject. In the coda, which is of sufficient length to balance the recapitulation against the elaborate exposition, the syncopated and triplet themes are turned to impressive account in octave passages between the soloists.

The themes of this Concerto are splendidly diversified. Those of the first movement have been for the most part articulated in short phrase-lengths, but we now have in the *andante* a broadly flowing tune whose romantic quality is heightened by echoing calls on the natural horns and by a richly woven string texture to which the solo violin and cello do no more than contribute strands of greater lustre. There is much welcome contrast of key (as so often with Brahms through the interval of a third, from D major to F major) and for further variety a new theme is assigned to the woodwind –

one whose suave thirds and sixths are strongly suggestive of the German folk-songs Brahms loved so well. The texture now begins to open out, and the two soloists share a swaying, flexible theme which leads them on to decorate with graceful semiquavers the smooth crotchet theme resumed by the woodwind. The pizzicato chords interpolated by the orchestral strings add a charming touch. A splendid series of modulations, the opening horn-signal reproduced with the additional brilliance of trumpets, and a cadenza, brief but fabulously difficult, for the soloists are landmarks on the way back to a subtly-varied repetition of the broad string melody. The poetical coda alludes to all the themes previously heard in the movement.

In the rondo finale the cellist is again the leader. Its main theme depends for lively articulation on skilful management of the bow, as Joachim was at pains to demonstrate to the composer: the bowings given in the score are Brahms's, nevertheless, though they are at variance with those recommended by Joachim. The passages leading to the first episode – or rather to the second subject as the movement is really in a sonata-rondo form – are made up of humorous interchanges between the soloists, involving hair-raising stopped intervals, and double stops are also prominent in the new C major theme. Shortly afterwards, the cellist's attempts to resume the principal (A minor) tune meet with disrespect from his colleague, who cuts across it with a contrasting rhythm, and from various members of the orchestral woodwind, who contrive to reduce the theme to isolated notes and rhythmic scraps; but out of these remnants suddenly emerges a vigorous new theme, with strong Hungarian-gipsy colouring, and elaborated by the soloists in the same tradition. The continuation of this idea, though less aggressive, also suggests eastern Europe in its syncopated lilt, and likewise lends itself to bravura variations. The main rondo theme returns in due course, works round to a sonorous recapitulation of the second subject (A major) and remains in that key for a coda wherein lively orchestral dialogues are enveloped in brilliant passages for the soloists. The scoring of the last few pages of the Concerto is of extraordinary delicacy, with solo string figures projected across woodwind and horns, while the orchestral strings are virtually silent until the closing tutti.